UNDERSTANDING THE
BLACK LIVES MATTER MOVEMENT

THE POLICE AND EXCESSIVE USE OF FORCE

by Philip Wolny

BrightPoint Press

San Diego, CA

BrightPoint Press

Content Consultant: Jennifer Cobbina, Associate Professor, Michigan State University, School of
Criminal Justice

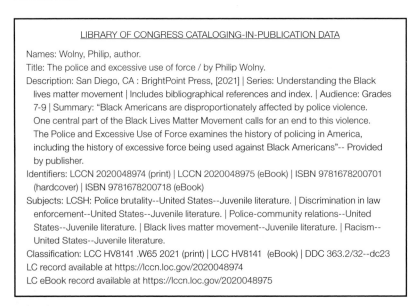

LIBRARY OF CONGRESS CATALOGING-IN-PUBLICATION DATA

Names: Wolny, Philip, author.
Title: The police and excessive use of force / by Philip Wolny.
Description: San Diego, CA : BrightPoint Press, [2021] | Series: Understanding the Black
    lives matter movement | Includes bibliographical references and index. | Audience: Grades
    7-9 | Summary: "Black Americans are disproportionately affected by police violence.
    One central part of the Black Lives Matter Movement calls for an end to this violence.
    The Police and Excessive Use of Force examines the history of policing in America,
    including the history of excessive force being used against Black Americans"-- Provided
    by publisher.
Identifiers: LCCN 2020048974 (print) | LCCN 2020048975 (eBook) | ISBN 9781678200701
    (hardcover) | ISBN 9781678200718 (eBook)
Subjects: LCSH: Police brutality--United States--Juvenile literature. | Discrimination in law
    enforcement--United States--Juvenile literature. | Police-community relations--United
    States--Juvenile literature. | Black lives matter movement--Juvenile literature. | Racism--
    United States--Juvenile literature.
Classification: LCC HV8141 .W65 2021 (print) | LCC HV8141 (eBook) | DDC 363.2/32--dc23
LC record available at https://lccn.loc.gov/2020048974
LC eBook record available at https://lccn.loc.gov/2020048975

CONTENTS

AT A GLANCE   4

INTRODUCTION   6
"I CAN'T BREATHE"

CHAPTER ONE   12
WHAT IS THE HISTORY OF
POLICE BRUTALITY?

CHAPTER TWO   28
HOW HAS BLM CHALLENGED
POLICE BRUTALITY?

CHAPTER THREE   46
HOW DID THE MOVEMENT CHANGE
IN 2020?

CHAPTER FOUR   60
WHAT'S NEXT FOR POLICING?

Glossary   74
Source Notes   75
For Further Research   76
Index   78
Image Credits   79
About the Author   80

AT A GLANCE

- Police use of excessive force is the use of more violence than necessary in a situation. This issue has had a significant impact on Black Americans.

- Policing in America has some of its roots in the slave patrols of the 1800s. After slavery ended, Black Americans were still subjected to discrimination and police violence.

- The Black Lives Matter (BLM) movement began in 2013. Activists formed the group following the acquittal of George Zimmerman in the death of 17-year-old Trayvon Martin. The movement protests racism against Black people, including police violence.

- Eric Garner, Michael Brown, Oscar Grant, Tamir Rice, Freddie Gray, Breonna Taylor, Elijah McClain, and George Floyd are among the Black people whose deaths in police incidents have drawn attention to the problem of excessive force.

- The 2020 death of George Floyd led to a massive protest movement and calls for police reforms. The BLM movement became the largest civil rights movement in US history.

- Banning choke holds, improving training, and requiring body cameras are among the police reforms that have been suggested and tried.

- Some people have supported defunding the police, meaning moving money from police departments to other social services.

"I CAN'T BREATHE"

Police in Staten Island, New York City, arrested Eric Garner in July 2014. They believed he was selling cigarettes illegally. After Garner resisted arrest, Officer Daniel Pantaleo tackled him and held him in a choke hold. Garner said "I can't breathe" eleven times.[1] Then he passed out. A bystander recorded the events on video.

The phrase "I can't breathe" became widespread at protests in the years after Garner's killing.

Garner was not treated by paramedics.

He had a heart attack on the way to the

hospital. He later died. Protests followed

Garner's death. People wanted to know

why police were still using choke holds. They had been officially banned for years. They also asked why the police had to tackle Garner. Protests happened in many places around the United States.

Officer Pantaleo was investigated over Garner's death. But a **grand jury** said it would not **charge** him with a crime. Federal investigators spent five years looking into the case. Pantaleo kept his job. He worked desk duty instead of being on patrol. A New York Police Department (NYPD) investigation led to his firing in 2019. He later sued to try to get rehired.

Many New Yorkers protested against the NYPD after the Eric Garner incident.

PROTESTING EXCESSIVE FORCE

Garner's death is one of many cases of

violence against Black people. The Black

Lives Matter (BLM) movement was born

in 2013 in response to such incidents.

It especially focuses on police use of excessive force. BLM now has dozens of official chapters in the United States and around the world. It has millions of supporters. When police kill people, BLM activists often protest. They push for changes to policing. They also demand that the officers responsible be punished.

People have protested and worked to change policing in America for decades. But in 2020, high-profile incidents of police violence happened. The BLM movement grew larger than ever before. Widespread protests show that policing is one of the

Major protests in 2020 drew more attention than ever before to issues with American policing.

most important issues in today's society.

Yet change has been slow. Many people

disagree over how to **reform** policing.

CHAPTER ONE

WHAT IS THE HISTORY OF POLICE BRUTALITY?

S ome early US police forces began as slave patrols. These patrols worked in the South in the early 1800s. They caught, beat, and returned enslaved people who tried to escape slavery. They also punished those who refused to work.

An illustration from the 1800s shows a member of a slave patrol catching an enslaved person who had escaped slavery.

In the 1800s, America's cities grew bigger and more crowded. Boston, Massachusetts, founded the first modern police department in 1838. Back then, there was rarely justice for victims of excessive force. Black people and other people of

color were targets of violence.

The United States fought the Civil War

from 1861 to 1865. The South had tried to

break away from the rest of the country. It

did this to continue the practice of slavery.

The North won the war. The country

THE NIGHT WATCH

The American colonies had something called
a night watch. Night watchmen walked around
towns at night. Their job was to prevent crimes
and protect property. They also watched out
for fires. Boston was the first big city to have
a night watch. It began in 1636. Most early
watchmen were unarmed. Some of them got
the job as a punishment.

became whole again. The United States

abolished slavery after nearly 250 years of

the practice.

Free Black Americans hoped to finally

enjoy their full rights and freedoms. But

many states passed unfair laws that

prevented this. These were called Black

Codes. They denied Black people legal

rights such as voting and freedom of

employment. Breaking these laws could

lead to imprisonment.

Later rules called Jim Crow laws

continued this discrimination. These laws

established different rules for Black and

white people and were in place in many states. Still, Black people in the South experienced some of the worst racism and hate. Police forces often targeted and abused them.

A racist hate group called the Ku Klux Klan (KKK) formed. It harassed and attacked Black people. It used bombs, mob violence, and lynchings to preserve control over Black people. In many communities, the Klan had close ties to police. Many members were police officers themselves.

In the 1910s, many Black Americans left the South. They wanted to find better jobs

Members of the KKK paraded openly in the 1920s in Pennsylvania and in many other states.

and lives. They also fled racial hatred and

discrimination. They moved to northern

cities such as New York; Chicago, Illinois;

and Detroit, Michigan. However, racism

was still a fact of life. Laws and customs separated people of color from white people in public spaces. This was known as segregation. Like in the South, northern police often treated Black people harshly.

A LONG-STANDING PROBLEM

Excessive force was in the news more than a century ago. In 1910, an editorial from the *Los Angeles Herald* talked about the issue. It said, "Not a week passes without some new instance of the injury or death of a prisoner somewhere in the United States." Police often stopped or arrested people for no reason. People were beaten or abused in jail. Police used torture to make people confess to crimes.

Quoted in Sarah Brady Siff, "Policing the Police: A Civil Rights Story," OSU Origins, May 2016. www.origins.osu.edu.

A LONG AND HARD ROAD

After World War II (1939–1945), many Black Americans joined the civil rights movement. They demanded equal voting rights. They also wanted equal access to public facilities, such as water fountains and lunch counters. The movement protested for good jobs and fair housing too.

The civil rights movement brought about important changes. The federal government threw out unfair rules that blocked voting rights for Black people. It made racial discrimination illegal in jobs and housing.

Protests helped spread the message of the civil rights movement. Police often cracked down harshly on protests. They used dogs and fire hoses on peaceful protesters. They also beat protesters and did not protect protesters from violent mobs. TV news programs showed footage of this violence. This helped shift public opinion in support of the protesters.

Even after the successes of the civil rights movement, police brutality continued. This included false arrests, harassment, and shootings. These actions led to further protests and even riots in the late 1960s.

Police used dogs to attack a fifteen-year-old boy in Alabama in 1963.

POLICE BRUTALITY IN THE VIDEO ERA

Years before smartphones existed, a video

tape recorder changed history on March 3,

1991. A witness secretly filmed Los Angeles

Police Department (LAPD) officers. They

were beating unarmed motorist Rodney

King. The officers had pulled him over after a highway chase. They struck King dozens of times with their **batons**. They also shocked him with a stun gun. Local media broadcast the tape.

The tape shocked and angered people in Los Angeles and nationwide. The King beating even made international news. Many Black Americans knew this kind of police abuse happened. But now it was recorded on camera. Activist, rapper, and author Sister Souljah talked to the *Los Angeles Times* about this in 1992. She said, "Police violence is a regular event in the

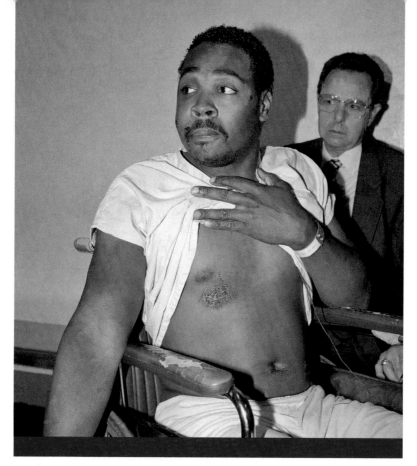

Rodney King showed reporters one of the injuries he suffered during his beating by LAPD officers.

Black community. It's as regular as brushing your teeth. The police have a hostile attitude toward men in our community."[2]

The next year, the trial of the officers ended. The jury found none of them guilty.

The California National Guard was sent in to help restore order during the rioting that followed the verdict in the Rodney King case.

People in Los Angeles and around the country were furious. The jury's decision sparked several days of protests and riots in Los Angeles. A total of 63 people died.

"THE MORE THINGS CHANGE . . ."

Another key incident happened in 2009. Police fatally shot Oscar Grant in Oakland, California, in the early morning of January 1,

2009. It happened at a train station. Witnesses filmed much of the event.

Officer Johannes Mehserle was the shooter. Another officer, Anthony Pirone, held Grant to the subway platform floor with a knee. Grant's family later said that Pirone also struck Grant. Video showed Mehserle pulling out his gun and shooting Grant in the back. Mehserle later claimed he panicked. Mehserle said he thought he had pulled out his Taser, a weapon designed to shock people without killing them. Grant died hours later. A jury convicted Mehserle of **manslaughter**. He served eleven

Protests about the killing of Oscar Grant predated the creation of the BLM movement.

months of a two-year sentence. Marches

and protests happened in Oakland before

and after his trial.

SMARTPHONES AND POLICE VIOLENCE

Protesters have continued to speak out

about excessive force. In the years after the

King incident, cameras became smaller and cheaper. This made it easier for people to capture incidents on video. In the 2010s, smartphones became popular. Now nearly everyone had a video camera.

Smartphones changed the number of people who see the use of force by police. Before then, a victim might have reported an officer's actions. It was often his or her word against the officer's. With smartphones, there can be a clear recording of the events for everyone to see.

CHAPTER TWO

HOW HAS BLM CHALLENGED POLICE BRUTALITY?

In February 2012, a Florida man named George Zimmerman killed unarmed Black teen Trayvon Martin. Zimmerman was a member of a neighborhood watch group. He confronted Trayvon. He thought Trayvon looked suspicious. No one knows exactly

Some protesters noted Trayvon's hoodie, saying that he had been seen as suspicious in part because of that common piece of clothing.

what happened. There were no cameras.

Zimmerman later said there had been a

struggle. Zimmerman shot Trayvon.

Authorities took a long time to charge

Zimmerman. Many people believed that

police and the courts acted slowly because of Trayvon's race. In 2013, a jury **acquitted** Zimmerman. It believed Zimmerman's story of self-defense.

The case upset many activists, including Alicia Garza. She wrote a Facebook post. It said, "Black Lives Matter." Along with Patrisse Cullors and Opal Tometi, Garza formed a group called Black Lives Matter.

BLM GROWS INTO A PROTEST MOVEMENT

BLM calls for an end to anti-Black violence. As part of this goal, BLM protests police killings of Black Americans. Organizers

Many protesters blamed systemic racism for the problems that BLM was working to solve.

started BLM branches in many cities. They

brought attention to police brutality and

systemic racism. Systemic racism is racial

bias present in society, including in areas

such as education, health care, and the

justice system.

Two cases made news in the summer of 2014. One was Eric Garner's killing in New York in July. The second happened in August in Ferguson, Missouri. Police officer Darren Wilson stopped Black eighteen-year-old Michael Brown. Brown was with a friend, Dorian Johnson. Wilson told Brown and Johnson to move from the street to the sidewalk. Brown and Johnson refused.

What happened next is unclear. The officer and Johnson told different stories. Johnson said that Wilson grabbed Brown by his neck and then shot him in the hand.

BLM protesters in Washington, DC, in 2014 used the name of Brown in their demonstrations.

He said the young men were afraid for their

lives and they both ran. Johnson stated that

Wilson shot Brown in the back. Johnson

said Brown then turned around and raised

his hands to surrender, but Wilson shot him. Investigators found that Brown had not been shot in the back.

Wilson told investigators that Brown punched him through his car window and tried to take his gun. Then, after he got out of the car, he said that Brown charged toward him after a short chase. Wilson fired twelve bullets, at least six of which hit Brown.

Some witnesses said that Brown had his hands up. They believed he said "Don't shoot" before Wilson killed him. Investigators determined he likely didn't put

Protesters in Ferguson soon spoke out about what had happened to Brown.

his hands up. But "Hands up, don't shoot"

became a popular slogan. Thousands

protested in Ferguson. There were peaceful

marches and demonstrations. Riots soon

followed too.

Local police responded in an effort to

stop the destruction. Both protesters and

journalists covering the protests complained about brutal police treatment. Police fired tear gas and rubber bullets. These weapons affected rioters, peaceful protesters, and journalists alike.

Protesters wanted Wilson to be charged with murder. They also wanted Ferguson's police chief to resign. Three months later, a grand jury decided whether to indict Wilson. A county attorney presented the case's evidence to the jury. Critics believed the attorney did a bad job. His family had close ties to the police. Critics said he showed confusing evidence on purpose. This would

Police take a protester into custody during the unrest that roiled Ferguson following the grand jury decision.

make indictment less likely. The grand jury decided not to indict Wilson. Protests erupted again.

ISSUES IN POLICING

The events in Ferguson made people think more about problems with policing.

Some people pointed to the issue of police militarization. The federal government had given police military equipment and

HAMMERS AND NAILS

Writer Radley Balko has covered police issues for many years. He once wrote about a famous quote: "If your only tool is a hammer, then every problem looks like a nail." Balko noted how military gear became popular among police. This started in the late 1960s. Around the same time, police began enforcing drug crimes more harshly. Balko said, "Soon, just about every decent-sized police department was armed with a hammer. And the drug war would ensure there were always plenty of nails around for pounding."

Quoted in Eric Schansberg, "The 'Militarization of Mayberry.'" Courier-Times, September 1, 2020. www.thecouriertimes.com.

vehicles. Armored vehicles and military-style weapons made some police officers begin to resemble soldiers. Critics said this made police feel more like an occupying army than officers protecting the community.

Another issue was officers' relationships with communities. Many officers do not live in the cities they patrol. They often live outside them in suburbs or small towns. This may lead them to think of people in the city as threatening.

Bias against Black Americans and other people of color is another big problem. Even police of color may hold such negative attitudes. They might see Black Americans as more dangerous. This bias can make cops treat them differently. This includes using deadly force. A 2019 study found that Black people are 2.5 times more likely to be killed by police than white people.

POLICE OR WARRIORS

Some people argue that training can play a role in how officers interact with the public. Police training may emphasize conflict rather than peaceful solutions. Officers point to the dangerous, unpredictable nature of their job. But critics suggest that warrior-style training promotes an aggressive mindset. They say this mindset can lead to violence.

CAUGHT ON VIDEO

Widespread cameras have made it harder to cover up excessive force incidents. Videos end up on the news. They spread on social media. They sometimes help victims get justice and inspire protests.

In November 2014, someone called the police on a Black twelve-year-old boy. Tamir Rice was playing in a Cleveland, Ohio, park with a toy gun. The caller said the person looked like a child, and they thought the gun was "probably fake."[3] This information was not passed along to the officers who arrived. Video showed them shooting Tamir

Memorials around the country, such as this one in Wisconsin, honored Tamir Rice and other victims of police violence.

just seconds after arriving. A grand jury

didn't indict the officer who shot Tamir,

indicating it felt the shooting was justified.

Protests followed the shooting and the

jury's decision. Black protesters wanted

answers. They felt their children were in

greater danger from police than white

children were.

Another **viral** video of a police shooting was taken in April 2015 in North Charleston, South Carolina. It helped one Black man's family get justice. Officer Michael Slager pulled over Walter Scott for a broken taillight. Slager shot Scott. He claimed Scott had struggled for his Taser and that he feared for his life.

However, a witness recorded the incident. His video showed Slager shooting Scott in the back as he ran away. Slager pleaded guilty to violating Scott's civil rights. In exchange for this plea, murder charges and other charges related to the case were dropped. Slager was sentenced to twenty years in federal prison.

Without video, police violations are hard to prove. More BLM protests and riots happened after the death of Freddie Gray in April 2015. The incident happened in Baltimore, Maryland. Police arrested Gray for having a knife. They put him in a van. They were supposed to strap suspects in safely. This was a new rule. Baltimore's police had a bad reputation for "rough rides." Rough rides are when police drive a vehicle violently. This is done to hurt a suspect who is not wearing a seatbelt.

Protesters as far away as Los Angeles, California, protested the death of Freddie Gray following his injuries in police custody.

Gray suffered a severe spine and neck injury. He died in the hospital seven days later. The officers were charged. But it was hard to prove what had happened. None of the officers were convicted for Gray's death.

CHAPTER THREE

HOW DID THE MOVEMENT CHANGE IN 2020?

In the 2010s, BLM continued fighting for change. More stories of police abuse came out. In 2020, another viral video spread like wildfire. This time it was from Minneapolis, Minnesota. BLM would soon grow larger than ever.

Illustrations and photos of George Floyd became common at protests as anger rose over his death in police custody.

Minneapolis police arrested George Floyd

on May 25, 2020. A shop worker had said

Floyd had used a fake bill. Four officers

responded. Floyd resisted being put in the

police car at first. He said he was afraid of

enclosed spaces. Floyd then apologized to the officers and was cooperative. He then fell to the ground. Officer Derek Chauvin put his knee on Floyd's neck. Floyd was held like this for about eight minutes. Bystanders filmed the incident. They yelled for police to stop. Floyd told officers "I can't breathe" several times.[4] He passed out. Chauvin only removed his knee when medics arrived. Floyd died.

Footage of the incident went viral. Large protests broke out in Minneapolis. They spread to other cities quickly. Most were peaceful. Some turned into riots.

NYPD officers detained protesters during demonstrations following Floyd's death.

PUSHBACK FROM POLICE

People filmed the protests and riots. Their videos showed many cases of excessive force. Police used riot control weapons. They didn't just target rioters, however. People were angry because police attacked many peaceful protesters as

well. Rioters were often mixed closely with

peaceful protesters.

Police used rubber bullets. One journalist

lost an eye after a rubber bullet struck her

LESS-LETHAL WEAPONS

Police use a variety of weapons. Some of them
are meant to break up dangerous crowds, such
as those at riots. Tear gas is one of these. It is
very painful. It temporarily blinds the person,
makes it hard to breathe, and burns the skin.
Police fire tear gas canisters into crowds. Police
also use pepper spray and rubber bullets.
These weapons are not meant to seriously hurt
people. But it is possible for them to injure or
even kill. This is why they are called less-lethal
rather than nonlethal weapons.

face. Police said it was difficult for them to tell rioters and journalists apart.

Officers used weapons like batons too. Some officers said they were only defending themselves after protesters threw rocks and bottles at them. But using these kinds of tactics made the public angrier.

NO-KNOCK RAIDS AND BREONNA TAYLOR

Another incident in 2020 highlighted the dangers Black people can face from the police. The events would become even more widely known during the summer protests. In Louisville, Kentucky, police

Police used a wide variety of weapons to control crowds during protests after Floyd's death. Many people believed they used excessive force.

broke into Breonna Taylor's apartment

on March 13, 2020. The police were

investigating Taylor's ex-boyfriend. They

thought he might have had drugs delivered

to Taylor's apartment.

Taylor was sleeping at home alongside

her boyfriend, Kenneth Walker. Police

arrived. They later said they announced themselves, though Walker and some neighbors said they did not hear this. The police were not in uniforms. Walker had a gun, and he fired at the police. He said he thought it was a home invasion. Police fired back. They shot thirty-two rounds. Several hit Taylor, killing her. Walker was unhurt.

An unannounced raid is also called a no-knock raid. This is meant to keep suspects from destroying evidence. Police say these raids keep officers safer. But they can go tragically wrong. In the Taylor case, it led to an innocent woman being killed.

A grand jury did not indict the officers involved for any crimes against Taylor or Walker. Instead, one was charged with putting neighbors in danger. Angry citizens said that Taylor's life was not valued.

BLM pushed the city government to change policing in Louisville. In June, the city council voted to ban no-knock search warrants. They also made it law that police must wear body cameras during raids. These new rules were known as "Breonna's Law." Kentucky senator Rand Paul introduced a similar bill in the US Senate. If passed, it would ban no-knock raids by

Taylor's death sparked widespread outrage and mourning.

federal law enforcement. The bill hadn't moved forward by the fall of 2020.

JUSTICE FOR ELIJAH

The 2020 protest movement also drew attention to an earlier incident of police violence. In August 2019, police stopped twenty-three-year-old Elijah McClain in Aurora, Colorado. He was walking home from the drug store with a bottle of iced tea. McClain wore a ski mask because he suffered from social anxiety, and he felt the mask protected him. He was moving his arms while listening to his headphones. This led to a stranger calling police. The caller said McClain looked suspicious.

Police said that McClain struggled with them. They said he reached for one officer's gun. All three officers said that their body cameras fell off, so there was no video. They held McClain down for fifteen minutes. One officer applied a choke hold. McClain vomited and passed out.

Demonstrators held a candlelight vigil honoring McClain in Los Angeles one year after his death.

The cameras did not capture video of the incident, but they did record audio. McClain could be heard crying and saying, "I can't breathe."[5] McClain had a heart attack in the ambulance and died three days later. Prosecutors did not seek charges against the police involved.

During the 2020 George Floyd protests, BLM activists in Colorado sought justice for McClain. Under public pressure, the three officers were taken off the streets and put on desk duty. Colorado governor Jared Polis ordered the state attorney general to

McCLAIN'S LAST WORDS

Police officers' cameras captured audio during the Elijah McClain incident. That included some of McClain's last words: "I can't breathe. I have my ID right here. My name is Elijah McClain. That's my house. I was just going home. I'm an introvert. I'm just different. That's all. I'm so sorry. I have no gun. I don't do that stuff. I don't do any fighting. . . . I just can't breathe correctly."

"Body Worn Camera Regarding the In-Custody Death of Elijah McClain," YouTube: Aurora Police, November 22, 2019. www.youtube.com.

investigate McClain's death. He said that the government should "criminally prosecute any individuals whose actions caused the death of Elijah McClain."[6]

McClain's family also filed a civil rights suit against police and paramedics. Their lawyers said that McClain was unarmed and had not committed a crime. They said he was stopped because he was Black. His family said that a lack of punishment for the officers would signal that it is okay for police to make more stops based on racial bias.

WHAT'S NEXT FOR POLICING?

In 2014, President Barack Obama launched the President's Task Force on 21st Century Policing. This group wrote a report that called for reforms. One idea was collecting more data on police shootings. Another was that police wear body cameras during all stops and arrests.

As technology has advanced, it has become easier to equip officers with small, lightweight cameras.

The report also suggested police training to de-escalate situations. De-escalation means calming things down. It means not approaching a situation aggressively. It also means doing everything to prevent using weapons.

8 CAN'T WAIT

In August 2015, some BLM activists launched Campaign Zero. It listed recommendations for police reforms. The goal was to reduce police violence. In 2020, the same activists launched a new campaign called 8 Can't Wait. This new project came after the death of George Floyd. The name referred to eight clear reforms. The group said these would reduce police killings.

The list included bans on using choke holds and shooting at moving vehicles. It would require police to de-escalate

STATISTICS ON POLICE KILLINGS

The group Prison Policy Initiative compiled data about police killings in certain wealthy countries. In 2020, it looked at the number of killings per 10 million people in the most recent year with data available. It then compared the countries. It found that the United States had by far the highest rate of police killings.

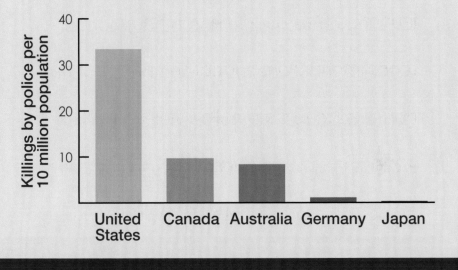

Alexi Jones and Wendy Sawyer, "US Police Kill Civilians at Higher Rates Than Other Countries," Prison Policy Initiative, *June 5, 2020.* www.prisonpolicy.org.

situations. Guns would be used only as a last resort after a clear warning. The reforms also included a responsibility to stop fellow officers from using excessive force.

ARE REFORMS WORKING?

Have body cameras, de-escalation, banning choke holds, and other reforms worked? Not everyone is convinced. Writer Dwayne David Paul tweeted his criticism of 8 Can't Wait in June 2020. He wrote, "All

A DIFFERENT MODEL OF POLICING

Policing looks different around the world. Norwegian police are not trained like soldiers going to war. Only a small percentage of those who apply are accepted. Recruits are highly trained and must pass tough tests in many subjects. They study society and police ethics. Some Americans believe US police should recruit and train like this.

of these policy proposals are on the books in many places and they do not reduce harm. #8CantWait is a series of toothless proposals undermining radical demands."[7]

Most big departments use body cameras now. However, police can and do turn cameras off. Equipment can fail. The public may never get to see footage, even for fatal shootings. Police departments sometimes take months or years to produce the recordings. Some studies show that cameras make some police less likely to use force. Others show they make little difference.

MIXED RESULTS

One case from Atlanta, Georgia, shows how body cameras can work. Rayshard Brooks fell asleep in his car in a fast food drive-through on June 12, 2020. Police arrived and questioned him. Brooks was drunk but talked peacefully with officers. He asked to walk home to his sister's house.

BODY CAMERAS

Many US police departments now require officers to wear body cameras. Body camera footage can help protect suspects or others stopped by police. They can also help police. The presence of cameras might make people behave better in these encounters. Cameras can also help judges and juries. Footage can show what really happened in a situation.

When the police tried to arrest him, he fled. Officer Garrett Rolfe shot and killed Brooks. The officers' body camera footage was released quickly. Rolfe was fired and charged with murder.

Rolfe had gone through de-escalation training just two months before the shooting. Some departments make training mandatory if an officer gets use-of-force complaints. Critics say that these steps are too small. Criminology professor Robin Engel told ABC News that de-escalation training is "a slow turn to change an entire field."[8]

Protesters set up a memorial for Brooks at the restaurant where he was killed.

Banning choke holds is a commonly suggested reform. However, there was an NYPD choke hold ban in effect when Eric Garner was killed with one. Police still used them. Statistics showed they were mostly used in Black neighborhoods. Officers were not punished for performing them.

Some cities that ban them have many exceptions for their use.

DEFUNDING POLICE

Some BLM activists think that recent reforms fall short. They want bigger changes. The 2020 protests made the public more aware of these issues. The idea of defunding the police became more popular in the summer of 2020.

A few activists want to get rid of the police entirely. But this is not what defunding means. Defunding the police means moving some money from police departments to other areas. The money could go toward job programs. It could

help with education or social workers.

It could pay for community centers. Cities

could fund health clinics, hospitals, and

mental health services. The idea is that this

spending would help prevent some crime

from happening in the first place.

In many places, police are first

responders in cases where someone has

a mental health crisis. Officers are often

poorly trained for this job. That is why such

calls sometimes end with mentally ill people

hurt or even killed. With some reforms,

social workers might respond to these calls

Protesters' calls to defund the police spread widely during the demonstrations in 2020.

instead. These people are trained to help

people work through mental health crises.

Activists believe this would be a better use of

funding that is currently used by the police.

RETHINKING POLICE

After the George Floyd protests, the

Minneapolis City Council planned to make

changes to the police. It wanted to shut down the Minneapolis Police Department.

The council was unable to take this step. However, it did move nearly $8 million from the $179 million police budget. This money would fund programs to help prevent crime. It would also pay for teams who could respond to mental health crises.

Activists and everyday citizens are likely to continue calling for change. The future of policing is unclear. It may depend on how today's reforms turn out. The problem of excessive force has existed in US policing

Protesters sought an end to a long history of police violence targeting Black people.

for generations. Today's protesters hope to

bring that long history to an end.

GLOSSARY

abolished
got rid of something

acquitted
found someone not guilty of a legal charge

batons
clubs used as weapons in law enforcement

charge
to formally accuse someone of a crime

grand jury
a group of people who decide if a person should be charged
with a crime

manslaughter
a legal term for killing a person without intending to

reform
to make changes to something in an effort to make it better

viral
spreading quickly over the internet

SOURCE NOTES

INTRODUCTION: "I CAN'T BREATHE"

1. Quoted in Erik Ortiz and Gabe Gutierrez, "For Eric Garner's Mom, Video of Man Pleading 'I Can't Breathe' to Police Is 'Reoccurring Nightmare,'" *NBC News*, May 26, 2020. www.nbcnews.com.

CHAPTER ONE: WHAT IS THE HISTORY OF POLICE BRUTALITY?

2. Quoted in Chuck Philips, "'Raptivist' Sister Souljah Disputes Clinton Charge," *Los Angeles Times*, June 17, 1992. www.latimes.com.

CHAPTER TWO: HOW HAS BLM CHALLENGED POLICE BRUTALITY?

3. Quoted in "Hear the 911 Call About Tamir Rice," *Los Angeles Times*, November 26, 2014. www.latimes.com.

CHAPTER THREE: HOW DID THE MOVEMENT CHANGE IN 2020?

4. Quoted in Maanvi Singh, "Floyd Told Officers 'I Can't Breathe' More Than 20 Times," *Guardian*, July 9, 2020. www.theguardian.com.

5. Quoted in Lucy Tompkins, "What You Need to Know About Elijah McClain's Death," *New York Times*, August 16, 2020. www.nytimes.com.

6. Quoted in Claire Lampen, "What We Know About the Killing of Elijah McClain," *The Cut*, August 11, 2020. www.thecut.com.

CHAPTER FOUR: WHAT'S NEXT FOR POLICING?

7. @DwayneDavidPaul, "#8cantwait is a series of toothless proposals undermining radical demands," *Twitter*, June 5, 2020. www.twitter.com.

8. Quoted in Erin Schumaker, "Reformers Push for De-Escalation Training," *ABC News*, July 5, 2020. https://abcnews.go.com.

FOR FURTHER RESEARCH

BOOKS

Samantha S. Bell, *The Rise of the Black Lives Matter Movement*. San Diego, CA: BrightPoint, 2021.

Duchess Harris, JD, PhD, *Black Lives Matter*. Minneapolis, MN: Abdo, 2018.

Clara MacCarald, *Rage and Protests Across the Country*. San Diego, CA: BrightPoint, 2021.

INTERNET SOURCES

Dakin Andone, "In One Week There Were at Least 9 Instances of Police Using Excessive Force Caught on Camera," *CNN*, June 8, 2020. www.cnn.com.

Christina Carrega and Sabina Ghebremedhin, "Timeline: Inside the Investigation of Breonna Taylor's Killing and Its Aftermath," *ABC News*, September 23, 2020. https://abcnews.go.com.

Chris Graves, "The Killing of George Floyd: What We Know," *MPR News*, September 11, 2020. www.mprnews.org.

WEBSITES

American Civil Liberties Union (ACLU): Police Excessive Force
www.aclu.org/issues/criminal-law-reform/reforming-police/police-excessive-force

The ACLU helps protect Americans' rights. This website offers resources from the ACLU around the topic of police use of excessive force.

Black Lives Matter
https://blacklivesmatter.com

The official Black Lives Matter website gives updates on BLM's actions throughout the country. It also shares the history of BLM.

Campaign Zero
www.joincampaignzero.org

Campaign Zero is a police reform campaign launched by activists to help guide cities and other governments with policy proposals on how to change policing.

INDEX

Balko, Radley, 38
Black Lives Matter, 9–10, 30–31,
    44, 46, 54, 58, 62, 69
body cameras, 54, 56, 60, 64–67
Brooks, Rayshard, 66–67
Brown, Michael, 32–34

choke holds, 6, 8, 56, 62, 64, 68
civil rights movement, 19–20

de-escalation training, 61, 62,
    64, 67
defunding police, 69–70

8 Can't Wait, 62–64

Floyd, George, 47–48, 58, 62, 71

Garner, Eric, 6–9, 32, 68
grand juries, 8, 36–37, 42, 54
Grant, Oscar, 24–25
Gray, Freddie, 44–45

King, Rodney, 22, 27

less-lethal weapons, 50

Martin, Trayvon, 28–30
McClain, Elijah, 55–59
Minneapolis, Minnesota, 46–48,
    71–72

no-knock raids, 51–55

Obama, Barack, 60

police history, 12–14
police in Norway, 64
police militarization, 38–39
protests, 7–8, 10, 20, 26, 30,
    35–37, 42, 44, 48–51, 69

Rice, Tamir, 41–42
riots, 20, 24, 35, 44, 48–51

Scott, Walter, 43
Sister Souljah, 22–23
slave patrols, 12
smartphones, 26–27
systemic racism, 31

Taylor, Breonna, 51–54

IMAGE CREDITS

ABOUT THE AUTHOR

Philip Wolny is an editor, author, and copyeditor hailing from Bydgoszcz, Poland, by way of Queens, New York. He currently resides in Florida with his wife and daughter.